CONSERVATION

A TRUE BOOK®

by
Christine Petersen

Children's Press®
A Division of Scholastic Inc.

New York Toronto London Auckland Sydney
Mexico City New Delhi Hong Kong
Danbury, Connecticut

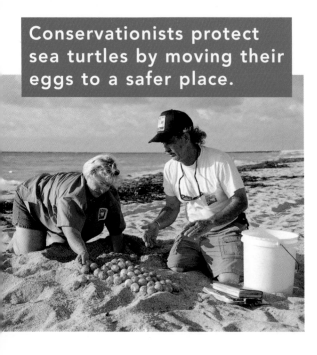

Conservationists protect
sea turtles by moving their
eggs to a safer place.

Reading Consultant
Jeanne Clidas
State University of
New York College

Content Consultant
**Dr. Jacqueline
Aitkenhead-Peterson**
University of New Hampshire

Library of Congress Cataloging-in-Publication Data

Petersen, Christine.
  Conservation / by Christine Petersen.
    p. cm. — (A true book)
    Summary: Describes some of the earth's natural resources, their
importance, and how they can be safeguarded.
Includes bibliographical references (p.   ) and index.
  ISBN 0-516-22805-6 (lib. bdg.)   0-516-21939-1 (pbk.)
  1. Conservation of natural resources—Juvenile literature.
[1. Conservation of natural resources.] I. Title. II. Series.

S940.P48 2003
333.7'2—dc22
                                        2003018344

1 2 3 4 5 6 7 8 9 10 R 13 12 11 10 09 08 07 06 05 04

Contents

Planet Earth

The Living Planet

Nine planets revolve around our Sun, yet only one contains life. That planet is your home, Earth.

Living planets are rare because life requires specific ingredients to survive. For life to begin, a planet must be close enough to a star (like our

The energy cycle for life is fueled by the Sun.

Sun) to get plenty of light—but not so close that the heat scorches it. Sunlight provides the energy that plants and some types of bacteria need to make their own food. In turn, animals eat plants, microscopic creatures, and other animals. This food web is one of the reasons that millions of species, or different kinds of living things, can share our planet.

Living planets also need an **atmosphere.** The atmosphere is an air bubble that contains a particular mix of chemical elements, the most common of which are carbon, nitrogen, hydrogen, and oxygen. Hydrogen and oxygen often join together, forming water molecules. Carbon, nitrogen,

and water move from the atmosphere to the land, through the
bodies of living things, and
back to the atmosphere. This
constantly repeating process is
called a cycle. For millions of
years, this cycle has maintained
a healthy environment that's just
right for life to thrive.

Humans are part of the living
planet Earth, but we sometimes
harm it. Today there are more
than six billion people—that's
more than twice the population
in 1950. Such a rapid increase in

An increasing number of people on Earth affects our natural resources.

population means that water and air may be **polluted** or used up more quickly than they can be **recycled**. Plants and animals are crowded out of their homes by our cities and farms, and wilderness areas are shrinking.

Rows of houses take over the landscape.

The solution to these problems is **conservation**. For humans, conserving means using only what we need and keeping our environment clean so that Earth's cycles may continue to work as they always have.

Earth's Fragile Resources

Air, water, and trees are called **renewable resources** because nature recycles or regrows them. That doesn't mean we can be careless with them—it means that if we use renewables wisely, Earth can replace them.

Large amounts of water are stored in glaciers, or huge masses of ice.

Water provides a good example. Ninety-nine percent of the water on Earth is either salty or frozen. That leaves only 1 percent that can be used by humans. Rain and snowmelt usually refill rivers, lakes, and underground water supplies, but overuse can cause them to dry up. Fertilizers, sewage, and trash can pollute our water. Polluted water is harmful to humans and deadly to animals and plants living nearby.

Water pollution harms organisms and affects our drinking water.

The air around us remains healthy only when it contains the right balance of chemical elements. Factories, cars, and the burning of coal and wood release dangerous toxic gases such as carbon monoxide, sulfuric acid, and nitric acid. These gases rise high into the atmosphere. When polluting chemicals mix with water in the atmosphere, they fall as acid rain that can poison plants and wildlife.

Trees damaged by acid rain

Fossil fuels (oil, gas, and coal) and minerals such as gold, iron ore, and diamonds are examples of **nonrenewable resources** that we use often.

Mining operations (above) move huge amounts of earth in order to extract minerals, such as copper and diamonds (left).

These materials are called nonrenewable because they exist in limited amounts—once they are used up, they cannot be replaced. Another problem with nonrenewable resources is that they are usually formed far beneath Earth's surface, so we must dig them out. Mining and oil drilling involve the use of dynamite and powerful chemicals that damage land and pollute air and water.

Fossil Fuels Ancient and Endangered

Millions of years ago, Earth was covered with tropical seas and swamps. When plants and animals died, their bodies sank into the muck. Heavy layers of sand and mud settled over them. Heat and pressure slowly removed water from the decaying bodies, leaving behind carbon in the form of hard coal or liquid oil and gas, known as fossil fuels. These fuels are used today to produce energy.

Fossil fuels—oil (top), coal (middle), and gas (bottom)—are formed from the remains of prehistoric plant and animal life. They are an important source of energy.

Conserving Natural Resources

Every person can make a difference by conserving natural resources. Walk or ride a bike around your neighborhood rather than using a car, which pollutes the air. Carpool to school to save gas. Turn off lights in empty rooms to save

Riding bicycles is a good way to reduce air pollution.

energy. Remind your parents to set the temperature in your house a couple of degrees lower in winter, and then put on an extra layer of clothes to warm up. In summer, open windows at night or use ceiling fans instead of the air conditioner. The average person uses about 50 gallons (189 liters) of water a day by washing dishes

Conserve water while washing dishes.

and clothes, showering, and using the toilet. Simple ways to reduce your water use include taking shorter showers and installing toilets that need less water to flush.

Conserving water means more than using less of it, however. It's also important to avoid polluting. For example, people often dump paint and car engine oil down household drains or into the street. This seems like an easy way to get rid of such chemicals, but it is dangerous for water supplies—anything that goes into drains and sewers eventually flows right into local rivers and lakes.

Landfills, deep holes where trash is buried, take up large amounts of land outside our cities. You can help reduce the amount of land taken up by landfills. Dump uneaten vegetables and fruits into a garden compost pile, add a

By composting, you can recycle yard and kitchen waste instead of sending it to a landfill.

little water, and turn it all over with a shovel every few weeks. Earthworms and insects will set up house quickly, eating the trash and turning it into a rich soil that plants love. Save plastic containers, aluminum and steel cans, cardboard, and newspapers to give to your local recycling center.

Recyclables ready for pick-up

Landfills can also be sources of pollution when dangerous chemicals from paint, batteries, or TVs leak into the ground and water. Instead of dumping such items in the trash, take them to a recycling center where they can be disposed of safely.

Scientists, industries, and governments must get involved, too. One important step is to reduce our dependence upon fossil fuels for

A scientist researches solar energy, or energy from the Sun.

electricity and car fuel. Scientists are looking for new, clean sources of energy to replace fossil fuels. Wind, water, and sunlight are just a few of the possibilities.

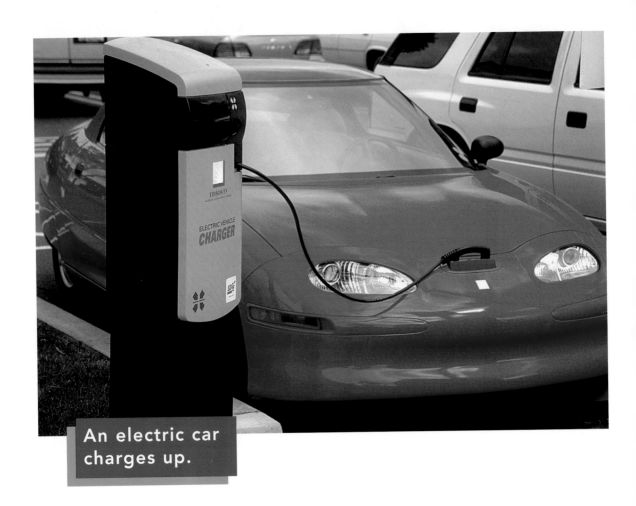

An electric car charges up.

Ethanol and electricity are already used in some cars in place of gasoline and cause far less pollution.

Conserving Species

Protecting the living things that share our planet is another important goal of conservation.

Anywhere you go, you're sure to find a wonderful variety of living things. So far, scientists have discovered more than 1,700,000 different species of plants, animals, bacteria, and

Researchers learn about new species by collecting samples from a forest.

other organisms living on Earth. Given time to explore hard-to-reach places such as deep oceans and tropical rain forests, scientists are sure to find many more species.

You might wonder why we should conserve all these species. The answer is that even the strangest creatures have jobs to do in nature.

Even cockroaches (top) and mosquitoes (bottom) have a role in nature.

For example, cockroaches are scavengers that clean up the environment by eating dead plants and animals, and male mosquitoes pollinate plants. Other creatures spread plant seeds across the landscape or till the soil. Plants produce oxygen and water, hold soil in place, and provide homes for animals. Humans can't do this work— we depend on other species to do it for us.

These medical vaccines were made from various plants.

Beyond all their benefits to nature, living things also help humans by providing us with food and medicine. Would you have guessed that a drug for treating breast cancer is found in the bark of yew trees or that mucus from the skin of poison dart frogs can be used to control pain?

About seventy species die off each day. At that rate, half of all Earth's species may be **extinct** by the year 2100. Today, most species die off because of human activities such as logging, mining, hunting, draining wetlands,

Large areas of forestland are continually being cleared.

and polluting water or air. This careless destruction of habitats and species leaves less wild nature for future generations and fewer resources for food and medicine.

Factories in the Forest

A logger cuts down a tree in a rain forest in Malaysia.

Every year, more than 36,000 square miles (93,240 square kilometers) of forest are cut down. That's an area larger than the state of Maine. People need wood for lumber and fuel, and use the cleared land for farming or building cities. Without trees and large amounts of healthy forest, however, most of the animals that live on Earth—including humans—could not survive. Trees and other plants are like living factories that take toxic carbon dioxide from the air and use it to make the oxygen we breathe.

Conserving Wilderness

A few thousand years ago, our entire planet was covered in marshes, grasslands, forests, and clean oceans and lakes. Today, people use up much of the land and water that was once so wild. As a result, many plant and animal species have lost their homes. The best way

Mute swans care for their young.

to conserve these species is to protect their habitats—the places where they eat, sleep, mate, and raise their young.

Creating parklands is one way to conserve nature, but it's only part of the answer. Parks are still affected by human activities. Logging takes place in many American parks. Oil companies drill in some wilderness preserves, and minerals are pulled from the soil in others. Cars, all-terrain vehicles, boats, and

As our planet becomes more crowded, few places remain where wild animals don't run into people.

even mountain bikes disturb wildlife and can cause damage to the environment.

Many of our modern parks are like islands, surrounded by civilization. These "islands" cannot grow larger because humans already use the land around them. Small parks can provide homes and food for only a limited number of species, and they cannot support animals such as wolves and mountain lions that need large areas in which to hunt.

One solution is to build natural "roads" called greenbelts between small preserves. Greenbelts allow wildlife to travel safely between parks without entering cities or crossing roads.

Conservation biologists believe that the best plan is to set aside large areas that are unbroken by roads, towns, or farms. This keeps wilderness in its natural state, as humans would have known it thousands of years ago. Such protection gives species, resources, and beautiful places a better chance to remain wild long into the future. Along the way, such careful planning gives our own species a better chance of survival.

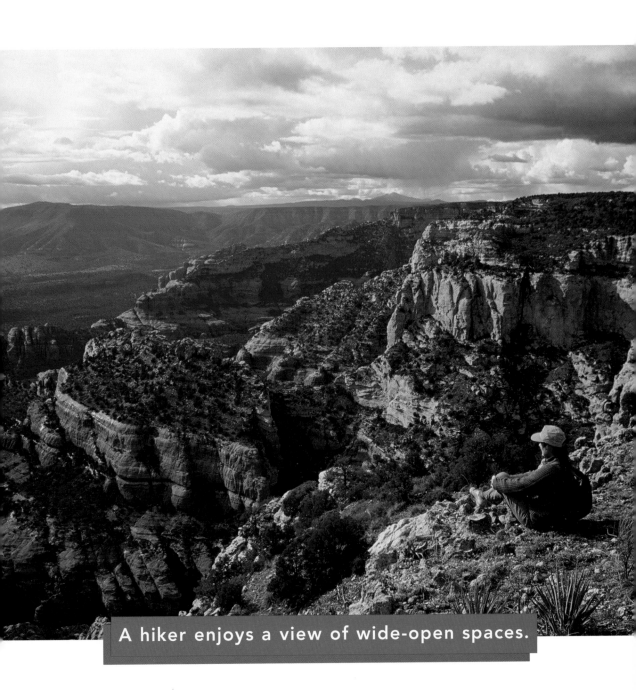

A hiker enjoys a view of wide-open spaces.

To Find Out More

Here are some additional resources to help you learn more about conservation:

 **Books**

Donald, Rhonda Lucas. **Recycling.** Children's Press, 2001.

Howson, John. **The World's Wild Places.** Raintree Steck-Vaughn, 1998.

Lasky, Kathryn. **Interrupted Journey: Saving Endangered Sea Turtles.** Candlewick Press, 2001.

Pringle, Laurence O. **Living Treasure: Saving Earth's Threatened Biodiversity.** Morrow Junior Books, 1991.

Organizations and Online Sites

World Wildlife Fund
1250 Twenty-Fourth Street, NW
P.O. Box 97180
Washington, DC 20090-7180
800-CALL-WWF
http://worldwildlife.org

This site includes a kids' page with screensavers and e-cards; quizzes, games, and activities; and an Action Kit full of ideas on how each of us can do our part to protect Earth.

National Geographic—EarthPulse
http://www.national geographic.com/earthpulse

This page includes up-to-date information on current conservation issues.

United States Fish & Wildlife Service Kids Corner
http://endangered.fws.gov/ kids/index.html

Students and teachers can use this site to investigate endangered species. The site includes games and links to other online resources.

Recycle City
http://www.epa.gov/ recyclecity

Explore an online "town" where pollution is reduced and trash is reused or recycled to create a cleaner environment.

Important Words

atmosphere the chemical gases that surround a planet, including air

conservation the protection of natural resources such as wildlife habitats, soil, water, fossil fuels, minerals, and species

extinct no longer existing or living

fossil fuels carbon products made from the remains of plants and animals that died millions of years ago, which can be used for fuel; includes oil, coal, and natural gas

nonrenewable resources materials such as fossil fuels and minerals that are formed by nature in limited amounts

polluted contaminated with harmful chemicals

recycled used again or naturally remade in nature

renewable resources resources, such as air and water, that are naturally recycled or regrown

Index

Meet the Author

Christine Petersen is a middle school science teacher who lives near Minneapolis, Minnesota. She has also worked as a biologist for the California Academy of Sciences, the U.S. Forest Service, the U.S. Geological Survey, and the Minnesota Department of Natural Resources, studying the natural history and behavior of North American bats. In her free time, Christine enjoys snowshoeing, canoeing, birdwatching, and writing about her favorite wild animals and wild places. She is a member of the Society of Children's Book Writers and Illustrators and is the coauthor of seven previous True Books.